The Hands in Exile

The Hands in Exile

SUSAN TICHY

RANDOM HOUSE NEW YORK

All rights reserved under International and Pan-American Copyright Conventions. Published in the United States by Random House, Inc., New York, and simultaneously in Canada by Random House of Canada Limited, Toronto.

Some of the poems were previously published in *The Antioch Review, Attaboy!, The Beloit Poetry Journal, The Black Warrior Review, Big Breakfast,* and *Blue Buildings.*

Grateful acknowledgment is made to the following for permission to reprint previously published material:

Alfred A. Knopf, Inc.: Excerpts from *The Measure of My Days* by Florida Scott-Maxwell. Copyright © 1968 by Florida Scott-Maxwell.

Forbes MacGregor and The Clan Gregor Society of Scotland: Historical detail adapted from *Clan Gregor.* Copyright © 1977 by The Clan Gregor Society of Scotland.

Library of Congress Cataloging in Publication Data
Tichy, Susan, 1952–
The hands in exile.
(National poetry series)
I. Title. II. Series.
PS3570.I26H36 1983   811'.54   82–48959
ISBN 0-394-52977-4
ISBN 0-394-71387-7 (pbk.)

Manufactured in the United States of America

9 8 7 6 5 4 3 2

First Edition

For Linda

Special thanks to Gaby, Alan, Ed, Avraham,
Yaacov, Eli, Salim, Mohammed, and Kearney
Charles, Kibbutz Shamir, Galil Elyon.

The National Poetry Series was established in 1978 to publish five collections of poetry annually through five participating publishers. The manuscripts are selected by five poets of national reputation. Publication is funded by James A. Michener, Edward J. Piszek, The Ford Foundation, The Witter Bynner Foundation, and the five publishers—Doubleday, E. P. Dutton, Harper & Row, Random House, and Holt, Rinehart & Winston.

The National Poetry Series, 1983

Joanne Kyger, *Going On* (Selected by Robert Creeley)
Jane Miller, *The Greater Leisures* (Selected by Stanley Plumly)
Donald Revell, *From the Abandoned Cities* (Selected by C.K. Williams)
Susan Tichy, *The Hands in Exile* (Selected by Sandra McPherson)
John Yau, *Corpse and Mirror* (Selected by John Ashbery)

Contents

Part One
The Hands in Exile

Painting the Fence   5

"During siesta . . ."   6

Consecration   7

Work   8

Irrigation   9

Artillery   11

The Hours   12

Defenses   14

"Writing on scraps . . ."   15

Lying on my Cot   16

In Kiryat Shmona   17

for Alan   19

for Avraham   21

At Dawn   22

Shabbat Morning   23

for Gaby 24

Dreaming I Am St. Augustine 25

Geology of the Huleh 26

Shabbat, Matah 27

"When I stop work . . ." 28

Staying 29

To an Irgun Soldier 31

"From now on . . ." 34

Benediction 36

Gaby at the U.N. Observation Post 37

Why We Don't Sleep 39

Tropical Storm 40

What They Say about Us 42

Identity Card 43

"A smell of gunpowder . . ." 45

To Part of Myself 47

Kovah Tembel 49

Two Cities, Three Loves 51

In an Arab Town 57

"The rich don't have children . . ." 59

At the Wailing Wall 60

Bargaining 62

The Hands in Exile 67

Volunteers 68

Part Two

Mare 73

Sauna 74

Altitude 76

Dreams of a Man without Children 78

Zen 79

Travel 80

Life Cycle of the Pacific Mermaid   82

No Matter   83

Talking from Inverness   84

A Meditation in Perthshire, Scotland   85

October   87

Florida Scott-Maxwell Helps Recite My Grandmother's Life   89

The Soul in the Valley of Kidron   94

Notes to Part One   96
Notes to Part Two   97

Part One

The Hands in Exile

Israel, 1977

And if thou wilt make me an altar of stone,
thou shalt not build it of hewn stone:
for if thou lift up thy tool upon it,
thou hast polluted it.

—E X O D U S 20:25

According to an apocryphal story, Jacob, not Moses,
built the first altar of undressed stone. He was
aided by the shamir worm, to which God gave the ability
to cut through stone. Formations in the Upper Galilee
and Golan Heights are still known as Shamir Granite.
Kibbutz Shamir lies in the Huleh Valley at the edge
of the Golan, in the narrow arm of Israel between the
Lebanese and Syrian borders.

Painting the Fence

We work close to the jeep, the M-16
barrel-up between the seats.
Rena'an says there's little danger.
The hills belong to the cows.

We work late into evening.
Rena'an counts to the monsoon
while I count hours of dark, hard as diamonds
rising off the town. We don't mind
that cows are stupid. They lick the paint,
nose the radio, and chew.

And out here the guns are loud,
louder than the steps of sleep
and the lack of sleep
as they circle
biting each other's tails.

The cows lie down. The calves sleep,
chins on their spines.
And it's better than sleep, this quiet
full of birds
and shuffling hooves and the paintbrush
sliding over rust.

"During siesta . . ."

During siesta a painter chisels landscapes
out of wood. He prints them one color on white:
barbed wire inside, outside desert guns.

Listen. Wild dogs
hunt down the rows of trees.
A steamy vitality centers on the irrigation system.

You are, for a moment,
set down inside *Justine.*
You are none of the characters,
just the voice: a city, a forest,
a sudden Greek slang in the wind,

the fine brown fingers of an artist
on the wooden stock of his gun.

Consecration

When the crop plane announces morning
sleep piles up in the back of the brain
dropped in a tangle out of silver wings
passing in the dark.
Everything captured is freed.

Pelicans circle the fish ponds,
their wings not yet colored
by dawn—hideous and innocent
as creatures from a dream.

It was easier than I thought,
painting at night: a sharp
bracelet of lights and wire,
the worship of bats in floodlights.

The jeep nosed up and down the ridges
where cows stood sleeping
on the old dirt-track border.
The hills themselves were in exile.

When a double moon rose,
the bright crescent and pale globe
hanging like permanent shellfire,
my skin barely tingled.

I trace with finger tips
the barbed wire cuts on my arms
and the white wings of the pelicans
blush, afraid to land.

Work

I just want to work today.
I just want to work all day today.
Fuck lunch. Let's paint
the haylofts. A young steer,
#879, wants to suck my sleeve.
O.K. Let him. Today
let's show the German city-girl
how to inseminate cows. Shit
up to the elbow. Cervix
like a rubber ball
caught through the rectum wall. Poor cow,
clambering up the cage walls
till they're sprung back. She's free.
What's the matter with me?
Here I am. Beautiful day.
Free clothes. Free dentist.
Ten feet from the flash
of a longhorn's eye.
I have the audacity
to remember someone else:
halfway around the world
his elbows are on some table. And that
is all I ever think about
at lunch. So that tomatoes pain me.
Siesta pains me.
Even tying my damn shoes pains me.
And when I stick my finger with a cactus thorn
that was sticking out of the blanket under my shoes
it serves me right
and it cures me.

Irrigation

Dust on my hair and face,
oil in the dust I can taste
when a truck has passed.
And the sting of grapefruit oil
in the small splinter-holes in my hands.
The smell of the plastic cooler
when I drink, water running down
my chin and throat and shirt,
disappearing in the heat.

A man told me his water truck broke down
in the Sinai, in one of the wars.
As long as convoys passed
he lived like a king
on cigarettes, brandy, chocolate,
and pictures of girls. Their nipples
made his mouth water
in spite of the dust.
The soldiers drank
till they sweated again
and he slept under his truck, dreaming:

The wars were over.
His country was an island
where men worked all day
pouring sand into the ocean.
Some schoolchildren were reciting:
How many people live in heaven?
What color is God?
Where do trees go when they leave the desert?
Why is it cold?

And he heard himself answering:
Don't listen to your own fears.
Pitch your tents in the shadow of running water.
It's cold in heaven.
And there are many gods in this green tree.

Artillery

Boom! That far-off door
opening and closing.

Shocked air falls off the ridges,
leaps up, stumbles,
throwing out its long voice like a noose.

And we're all caught.
It feeds us dust
from the battlefields, keeps us
in the singed air of shorted wires.
Our hair stands on end.

The words of our mouths
get trapped in our ears,
shaking.

And when the ground shakes
dust falls off the top shelves
like dust off a moth
when it stops eating our clothes
and flies away.

I keep my hands in my pockets
as if to say, "I won't touch
this tremor."

Or the grit between my teeth.
Or the damp between my legs.
I drink a glass of water fast

and smell the apple trees.
They are not blooming.
They are shaking
their fragrant leaves to the ground.

The Hours

The crop plane stalls its engines,
drops an octave and a hundred feet
into a zoom of poison,
plowing through sleep nose first.
That's dawn.

Noon is the whistle,
like a sword blade,
of passing jets.
They go nowhere.
They bomb nothing.
The papers say
no borders are ever crossed.

Dusk we mark by a rumble,
far away, noticed only
when a day's work is done.
The rumble is the animal that guards us.

So, what if I slept on the other side?
Right there, perhaps,
in that small twinkle of lights?
I'd stroke the black, shining hair
of the same animal
and feel safe.

This is peace.
It causes men to grow old. On women
the face of an olive leaf
coarsens
into cracked ground waiting for rain

or darkness.
We each lie down.
Wind lifts soil and branches,
lightening everything
but us.
It even blows the borders
back and forth above our heads:
at twelve we are in Israel,
at two we are not.

At five, when the crop plane
already revs its engines in half light,
we fall asleep and dream,
for half an hour,
that we climb the swaying ladder
to God's house.

Defenses

What's this? This
is a concrete bunker
in a blanket of bougainvillea.

And who are they?
Two lovers
from different countries.
One looks happy
and one looks sad.

And over here,
where the lovers
in their deepest inattention
might have strayed?

Barbed wire
and old machinery
rusting on the hillside.

We hope the enemy
will stumble
and swear at himself
in the dark.

And that smell?
Is that the flowers?

No, that is how we know
when they are shooting.
An odor of light
drifts toward us through the dark.

"Writing on scraps . . ."

Writing on scraps of paper, between jobs
and the cows' inquisitive breathing.

All the smells—of hay, shit, their bodies,
liniment, leather, and dust—

if any are missing I know it is a dream.
Scraps accumulate, innocent of verbs—

the scrape of a cow's lip on my arm,
the scrape of a pen on a dusty page.

Pause for a smoke—that smell
and the smell of paint. "From such work

no poetry comes," says an old man
who has done this half his life.

Lying on My Cot

The cigarettes taste like horseradish
but they're free. Bugs
leave holes in the rolling paper
going in and out.
Towns on the horizon go on and off.
The mosquitoes aren't so bad
since I let the lizards in.
With crickets, orange soda,
the big guns and small-arms fire,
it's peaceful, like thunder and popcorn
on the back porch
on a hot, Southern night.

Down below, a tractor driver
takes his turn at the gate. I hear him
check his weapon,
the spin of gravel when he turns,
the short *chuk* of a match.
One of his radios speaks code,
the other rock-'n'-roll: "Baby!"

I like to imagine the bugs
beating hell for fresh air,
tearing at huge walls of paper,
their teeth not fast enough,
their burned bodies traveling down my lungs.

Across this silence, Lebanon blooms
like an irresistible flower.

In Kiryat Shmona

The café man sure likes us, joins us,
says I'm a pretty woman.
Don't pay for the bottles.
Sit with your back to the border.
Spent shells make objets d'art, and besides
we want to touch them. October,
and the chance to leave
passes with the season of Deck Fare.

Poor men think they can make it here,
we're told. Nobody else will stay
except the foreigners and artists
and none of them look for jobs.
We wear our cleanest shirts
and drink—

That wide-eyed apple picker,
watch him order what he can't pronounce,
get drunk, in love with a table leg.
Hot damn, eh?
His cousin translates:
just because he doesn't know who he is
doesn't mean he isn't somebody.
Everybody wants to kiss. And no one mentions

the angles of the guns
or exact altitudes of the hills.
Those are intimate statistics,
like the sizes of our shoes. We talk
about the change of season, and home,
as if that were not someplace
we have left. Surviving

Kiryat Shmona is an Israeli border town, frequently shelled from PLO bases in Lebanon.

is the easy part, or so they say.
If you hear a mortar whistle
it's missing you. Stop running.
The one to fear is silent, invisible
from where you stand
at the exact end of a line.

for Alan

Flies gather on my pants leg.
An old *Time* covers half the window,
the half where I killed
my last three angry flies.
The boy from New Jersey says
the moon over the Golan means
life is not as it seems. A gun

is a collectivity of wood,
metal, and practice.
Reaching into the jeep one day
I feel the barrel,
a chill on my Adam's apple.

Avraham, the painter, says
my words are serpentine.
Over dinner he tells me
revolutions are only his ulcer.
God's first law was not
Thou Shalt Not Kill. It was
Thou Shalt Not Touch.

He shows me etchings
of boxes in the grass, their lines
rising and folding in the air.
They say: whatever grows here
we are something else.
He shows me the pen
that glides through ink,
leaving behind its absence.

Learn that, he says, and life
will be just as it seems.
The greatest danger,
the boy from New Jersey says.
The Japanese boy says nothing
when he throws his empty bottle at my head.

for Avraham

That is your death you are drawing,
that black box.
Some days it nestles in the grass.
On days of hope it levitates
or thins to a single line.

Those sudden curves,
bulging orange or red—
you feared them like a pair of fists.
But they were only the ulcers
eating morning and night.

There it is now—
that park bench in deep grass.
That shack
with its tilted but parallel walls.
And that, too, the peaked black cap
you are wearing.

Even after the last good-night
it shows
on the curved underside
of your eyelid,
a white square outlined
on the sleeping globe
of your eye.

At Dawn

I hesitate outside the door.
Ground fog lies on the irrigated land,
nothing but tall Lebanese cedars
showing their tips,
the windbreaks, the Japan
I would like to visit, Japan
of ink-wash and line.

Shabbat Morning

God, I am sorry.
The veterinarian from Haifa
will be here in the morning.
The cows must come down
from the Golan Heights today.

We do not pass a man in a prayer shawl.
We turn off the sprinklers
and ride between rows of trees,
the ears of the horses
parting a manmade mist.

Underfoot, the ground is warming.
Overhead, the sun waits with an axe.

    I promise when I walk
    to step where a cow has stepped,
    and when I ride
    to ride in line like an ant.

for Gaby

We're coming down from the old
border station, wading the cold stream.
The wings of the wild flamingo sun
are caught in the viny trees

and we begin to say to each other,
"I do not want to go home.
I have enough feet to walk on,
to walk far into the interior."

But this is neither Africa
nor Asia. This is a ghost forest,
a hinge, a place
of very hard work. And the axe

is a dream running through it,
a dream of a door
that opens from all sides
onto the shore of the sea.

We keep walking down from the border.
The June bugs sound like engines.
We keep walking our ankles
through the water, thinking,

"There never was a better place
for ambush."

Dreaming I Am St. Augustine

First a tree.
In its shade, cattle
and a stone wall.
A boy with a red face
holds water in a jar.
Then the wood
cut from the tree
bobbing in a sour pool.
The boy asleep,
his dreams billow out from a stone beneath his head.
Above him
on a knife without a hand
a ram
opens its stinking throat.
The boy wakes.
He points to me.
"You are a stone.
Whenever I wish
you turn to bread,
get up,
become a man."
He climbs into his tree.
The stones leap up.

Geology of the Huleh

Geese are invisible
but honk down at dark
into grass.

Though it's dry country
books describe
a great swamp, taken

drop by drop
and bug by bug.
They don't say where.

To Syria, perhaps,
spreading fever
like hatred from the wells.

Perhaps to darkness.
A pool of bad smells
waits there

for anyone who ventures
down, toward a gleaming
memory of sleep.

Shabbat, Matah

Long-legged wild dogs
startle down aisles of a dozen greens,
in and out of tractor ruts,
day-old, deep
in watered orchard ground.

Neither the guns
nor the different whispers
of grass, apple leaf, weed, and air
are heard on a working day.
Climb to the top of a McIntosh:

left and right the road
weaves through scrap metal, old cars,
plows, and wire, to the gate.
"It was all we could think of to do,"
they'll tell you. See

how each separate tongue of water
shaped a hill? Flyways change,
but slowly: a startled pelican
veers away from the McIntosh

and a silver fish hits ground so hard
I jump, heart fisting like knuckles
against the apples, sun-warm,
a hard, red armful on my breast.

Matah is a pear or apple orchard.

"When I stop work . . ."

When I stop work and rub my face
I rub soil of the Promised Land
into my skin.

Whose bones do you suppose
are filling my pores? Who smiles
in the dark crescents under my nails?
A soldier, or his shy, malarial bride?

> *Except a corn of wheat*
> *fall into the ground and die,*
> *it abideth alone.*

If I stayed here seven years
every cell would die
and grow again. I would be
Holy Land, all over

—except the brain, whose cells
are grains of sand in a rock fortress
imagined by tired travelers
to be the City of Peace.

And yet, my cheek
would not be more beautiful,
nor would this soil have yielded
one bushel of olives, one bough.

Staying

"There was no one to show us how," or so
the old Jews tell it.
                        From a seat
on the high, long island of Rome
that parts the cotton field,
both ridges are beachlike, beige
and baked-white.
                        In excavated rooms
I whisper to myself, nod
cracked-lipped agreement
with the homesick Legionnaires:
                                    ignore
whatever gods are up there
pouring wind and gun sounds.
                                    Lie down
and the air knits close, the grass
fish-scaled, blooming yellow
and pink.
            "As settlers
our hands were white.
We shed blood and planted grass.
In each hour, in each field,
we invented one year of the past."

And the caves are invisibly high
where Zealots sleep, those ridges
white, and manacled with heat.

All the view is sky and land,
joined at a line
where birds are always
suturing.
        "We learned
and now we understand.
When seed is small
you mix it in your palm
with sand."

To an Irgun Soldier

I.

One camel survives Jerusalem.
A dollar-and-half a ride, it lies
bored on the pavement
on the Mount of Olives, in front
of the library. Don't you remember?

El Lawrence was not in sight.
The two boys passed time
molding camel shit into enormous piles
with their bare feet. I had just
asked you if a man
remembers what country he died in.

You turned to face the synagogue.
"When blood is spilled, may it spill
on the outside walls." Your eyes
nested in their deep lines—from laughing
or from squinting at the sun?
Your lips embraced their cigarettes,
your tongue its poems . . .
And yes, yes, you helped me
get a job, a ticket, drinking
toasts to me, to you. But here

I work. And here
the hillsides wear their houses
like an old tattered shawl.
I build. But what I build
some other will knock down. It's simply

Ha Yorden—"that which falls."
And everything I see around me
falls—men, houses, hair
of a woman, tumbling from its combs.
If not by bombs, by wind.
And last of all, the sky.

Still, there are details—flecks
of mica in the soil, streaks of red
down certain blades of grass. By details
I remember this is more
than the dry course of our thoughts.

Just now, the hands you once compared
to white cups—unbreakable and pristine—
are oiling a pair of boots
with Vaseline. Once stylish,
the boots are French
and crudely painted black—an artist
would have had them for his models
if there were artists like that anymore.

And landscape? Days are cold.
The lake of miracles is gray
and placid as the sky. I've learned
to move slowly, to ask few questions
in these oil-and-mud-stiff pants.

I work.
And after work, I drink
until the memory of your hand falls
away, light as a shock
of wheat against my thigh.

When children come, noisy and pushing
through the chairs of this café,
I wrap my fingers tight
to a glass of Arab tea
and rum.

Ha Yorden—"that which falls"—is the Jordan River.

My feet
are so far away
they speak with another tongue.

2.

And yes, yes, maybe you didn't
blow that building up. Perhaps ships
approaching on the two seas
—salt and sand—collided.

That's your business—
knowing what no one knows,
not seeing what everyone sees.
I believe it. I believe

crows wish there were no animals
dead at the side of the road.
And among these men and women
seated at the café,

one of them loves another. The rest?
We made it up. Your hands are virgins.
And Israel, their bride, lies still
just under the face of the hill.

Out in the street,
where boys are cracking puddles
with their bare heels, ice shatters
like clapped hands between the walls.

The death of God was not like that.
The death of God was gradual,
a workman's shirt falling slowly to pieces.

"From now on . . ."

From now on I am a road
just reaching the top of a hill—
I go on but I can't see where.

Let rain fall. Let breath
condense on the dirty glass.
The present is my house
and my house is full of children.
I lift each one above my head, and shake out
the armies that fly from their mouths.

Some of the children speak plainly.
Some comb out their tangled hair.
Some pack the suitcase
they'll carry to the next life.

But what I love and what I hate—
I'm letting go of their hands,
those two poor twins.
Who will take them in?

The sun will shrivel, the rain distend,
and the wind will roll me over in her arms.
No one will know what size shoes
I was wearing, not even me.

It will be "the day of labor,
the night of gunfire" forever.
No decisions but the necessary ones.
And no more nights like this one.

From now on I am a road of stone,
hewn, and mortared to the hill.
When a man strikes his foot against my shoulder
let him swear, let him stoop to rub the bruise,

and rest where a cypress blocks the wind
like a shawled woman turning her back.

Benediction

Blessed is the busy man: his many deeds
follow like wives at his back.

Blessed more is he who achieves nothing:
nothing shall be burned on his behalf.

Blessed, as well, the woman
who never sleeps:

wine shall stain her teeth
and salt grass grow on her tongue.

Twice blessed is the soldier: his labor
keeps heaven and earth apart.

But blessed above all
are the ignorant:

their laughter is the thread of silk
we follow through the dark.

Gaby at the U.N. Observation Post

. . . *you find yourself always standing*
Between the much-praised landscape
And the one that praises it and explains it

—YEHUDA AMICHAI

I.

On the border
you're posed and poised as a model
who has no idea where she is.

You cross your legs. One elbow
rests on the telescope mount
where a newspaper is tucked
and folded: the news
is startling and old, news of a year
in which love joined hands with her sister
and both went down to death.

On the Day of Atonement
thirsty hands drank from the eyes,
and those who had nothing to grieve for
received a gift.

The gift you wanted? To win the world
by leaving it alone.

2.

You're not alone.

To one side, shadows of things that happened.
To the other, dreams that didn't come true.
The land is dry because of them. They live

37

on the surface of things, like gypsies,
drinking all the moisture from the air.

Here, give them a loaf of bread
and wine from an earthen jar. Say,
"This is no longer the border.
This is no longer the war." Tell them
in each of your four languages,

"I want to go home alone."
What if a man is waiting for you?
What if your body
could be his whole country—
two countries, for night and for day?

On the Day of Atonement
you painted your face with make-up
and walked to the top of the city wall.
Everyone saw you mourn
for having your hands and feet.

3.

Two hands, two feet—
you are never alone.

Out of your father's country
you marched
at the head of a million dead.

But when you tried to lead them
to the future
they ran back, disappearing
through a small crack in the earth.

Don't rub your toe in the dust
like that. Show respect.
Turn your face away from the wind
when it blows
their loose hair in your eyes.

Why We Don't Sleep

The shack will tremble
when tanks pass on the road.
I think of this, then try
to count them like sheep.

"At the ammunition dump
do not get out of the jeep." Syria
hangs a brown dust over the east.
Khamsin: it's not a sin

to kill your wife when it blows,
when weeds move like an earthquake
and everything is a sky.

Lights from the guard jeep
sweep the shack wall, bluish
like sun

on the black Bedouin dresses
of pock-faced women passed today
in small horizon towns.

When they turned toward us
their rhinestones,
set in red embroidery, flashed

like the half-dozen lights of their towns
that wink yes-no all night
under guns.

Rena'an is right:
the eucalyptus trees
make it hard to breathe.

Khamsin is a hot, dry desert wind.

Tropical Storm

One pink flash. Pink!
We are really hit
this time. We fall from bed, then
off the porches of the shacks
to gather
at the bolted bomb-shelter door.

Footsteps down the hill. A clatter
of gun barrels on gravel
we're sure. Isn't there
a radio for help? We're
barefoot. Who is that

coming? The man with the key?
The man with instructions?
Or should we flatten
into this scanty bush, take cover
under grass stems, behind
our nationality or shacks?

And is that fire rising
over the dining-room roof,
yellow as dawn, quick
as lizards? We've been told:

be useful. Already
on the first day of war
there is no getting out.
We stand our ground, muscles

taut in the damp air.
But we feel death
like a round hunger.
How fast it's eating up
our guts. Then

like a ripped seam down the sky
lightning shows
—for a heart beat—
the dining-room roof
intact, the moon
rising. A lover

sidles past us up the hill.
Nothing wets us but the rain.

What They Say about Us

Though they are good people
and you can't argue that

they bug me
just a little.

Argue. Let me.
You mean . . . ?

I don't mean. True.
It's not their attribute

but yours.
We have it.

Jesus!
All they care about.

I'll argue.
Jesus was a Jew.

Don't say that.
Jesus was a Jew.

Don't say that.
Jesus was a Jew.

It's true.
Don't say that.

Identity Card

For a living I pick apples.
No, that's not true. I could live
perfectly well without them.
I pick grapefruit, but my passion

is for tottering
on the tall, three-wheeled machine
I pilot through the branches.
The whole ocean is visible,
the ocean which is this orchard,
its tossed whitecaps of blossom
gone to fruit. We call it autumn

when the grass around the unpicked trees
is dry. Dew settles on the moon
instead. Its orange face
is the smile I wear in the dark.
Two weeks of that, then rain,
and then the war.

I'm not the only woman
and not the favorite. I work too hard
and drink my tea with sugar.
That makes you sweat, they say.
"In the army, sugar is not allowed."

So I heap more in my cup.
And I work, in the rainy time,
where no one wants to work: on the hills
with the rangy cows, the unswept mines,
and the dazed bull
honking his severed vocal cords.

More sugar! More smell of the diesel
mingling with grapefruit oil!
More nights polishing my old French boots!
Let the enemy reveal himself,
slyly, in the orchard,
or, wearing a clean shirt, at night.
This is all he will learn:

Name? A Polish village.
Rank? Apparently so.
And number? Try the number

on a letter that keeps coming back.
For a living I am insomniac
and drunk—all the time—
like a bee in a wet spring bloom.

"A smell of gunpowder . . ."

There are things which will never again
protect you.

—YEHUDA AMICHAI

A smell of gunpowder rises from the closed flowers,
and, from the valley, water with its smell of hoses.

I'm holding a stone in the dark,
sanding my calloused fingers on its skin

while the moon lights only
that which is far away—

the absence of orchards in plowed fields.

In the roving eye of the war
I'm an easy target, pale
by the dark square of my shack.

In the stone a second eye is fixed,
enclosed in a cool, crystal albumen.
The eye of Eden, perhaps.

And as for what was promised—
He said, "Touch not the fruit."
He said, "Touch not the stone."

The Devil himself
sleeps in the citrus groves.
I'm waiting for the wind

to nip through those branches
and sneak up under my clothes.

Even the flies are waiting,
clinging to me for warmth. And I feel safe

with the real guns, on the real border,
between two halves of the imaginary world.

With a little piece of grass between my teeth.

To Part of Myself

What's my business here, rising at dawn,
swimming through fog to the truck? All morning,

sweating a mixture of grapefruit oil and dust,
I can't remember. Then I remember

you as clearly as if you dawdled,
neither working nor resting, between these trees,

restless on this last day, folding up memories
like pieces of bread to live on.

To live *on*, and further on—
is that why you sent me away, why

you bathe me with water and sand,
with one and then the other, until

in spite of labor I am clean, so clean
my skin gives off an odor of night air?

The day has wandered to a close,
but dusk, huddling at the tree trunks,

has not yet entered the road.
I step out

with dust, oil, sweat, and bread
all stuck to my palms and my skin,

watching for the truck's twin lights
to come, eating up their own white tracks:

one's aimed askew, to mark it as a friend.
I recognize the touch

when you pick up your hands to hold me
at arm's length again.

Kovah Tembel

From months and snags and all the hours
it takes to get to Haifa on the bus
my last trousers have worn out.
I'm startled by the shape and size
of new ones. Have I changed?
Am I smaller now, and straighter?
Has my hair changed color
from the sun and from the rain?
The woman who cuts it asks. The friends

who take my work clothes
return the money they find
in several pockets. My French boots
fit no one. My bus ticket
has writing I have still not learned
to read. And on my back hangs everything:
my calluses, my photographs, the language
I learned to speak here—English
in a twisting sequence,
like a map of many countries.

These are my only stories: summer
when the only shade was behind my eyes,
and winter—the only blue
my knapsack nailed to the wall. Autumn,
in between, came suddenly, like this:
at eight o'clock, when we'd normally
shed everything snakes and decency
allowed, we had not even rolled down our socks.
And nights? The nights were long and full

The kovah tembel is the familiar blue kibbutz hat.

of distant thunder, like
a great grouse calling his love.
I also heard the small stuff—
very loud rain on the roof of the world.
Or, I could tell them this:
that on the last morning dawn opened
its first eye, and the tall cypress
flared on the gray sky, a black torch
held to all our faces:
those going, those staying, those

rolling over in their sleep.
I swept my shack. I hung the blankets
up to air. I left the cups, the teapot,
and a pile of blank paper behind.
No one will know me where I'm going
in my fool's hat, with my closed mouth,
and all this landscape in my head,
wild, but safe, fenced in
behind the lines on this page.

Two Cities, Three Loves

1. Student

My father once said
when he was praying on the stones:
Lower your eyes from the moon
& shun the sea & traveling!
—MAHMOUD DARWISH

Yet you, a good son, have followed me
as far as the farthest orange tree.
Moon glistens in your face: the sweat

of generations, thinned and hardened
on your delicate skin. "Teach me English
for two tongues,"—your way

of taking me in your arms. Far overhead
the stars are tiny handkerchiefs
waved at your departure.

You later, in your shy way, say
there is no sin on my part, lying
on the flat stones, picking cactus

from our clothes. I am still pure
to you, a ship of snow, sailing
through great darkness, like the moon.

As for your straying—*it is written*
somewhere, in some language. It means
they'll never tie you

to the single wheel of one tongue
wearing its rut in your soul.
Let your father search your face

for soil and rainfall of his stolen farm.
He sees no more than white heat-lightning
playing in your eyes. For him

there is one history, bounded by the sea.
For you—I taste the salt air melting
on your tongue. Lie still. Watch

the blossoms of the orange tree blow down
and skitter toward that line
where waves drop their silence

and the night sky shines up from wet sand:
All this is danger to a man already counted
with the dead. Feel in my touch

a veil of sand on your skin. Sing,
and the flat rocks of your country raise
their tips, like many serpents' tongues.

Even your laugh is a family laugh:
soldiers march, but under boots there grows
the thin green banner of the grass.

What did you think I could teach
in a prickly, swift caress? To taste,
with a closed mouth, the few mild drops

that fall from the moon's tipped glass? Pleasure,
you already know, is a soft, playful bite.
Pain is the next breath that you draw.

2. Soldier

Let me describe your eye
as it concentrates, taking aim:

black paint
dropped into blue water
where the beaches are covered with snow.

The faint pink lines
are my reflection, though you call them
memories. Your mouth is wet.

And blue, blue
is everywhere behind your head.

I know why women love you. Your breath
softens the wood your cheek is laid upon.

They, too, would like to be held
in your strong arms over the earth.

They would like to be feared and quick
and bite at the legs
of even those who survive you.

3.   Safad

What were you thinking,
turning my face to that strange light?
Night was falling for the last time,
quickly, and the lake rose toward us
through the dark that gathered
like an audience around its light.

See how easy it would be to separate
my body from what I am? Untie me,
and the history of my people
will fly off into the darkness
like a kite. Unravel the string.
I'll shrink back
past my childhood, past
the day I learned to walk
with a pound of smuggled bullets
in each shoe.

Safad is a city on the Lake of Galilee.

4. Widower

Grief is a white bird
and you don't find it on battlefields.
—M A H M O U D   D A R W I S H

"They told me, *marry again,*
when the seven men were dead,
piled like a lucky harvest
on the beehouse floor.

Their faces,
as like my own as brothers',
are seven pebbles lodged
between my brain and skull.

No, please! Don't lie down
here, on the grass beside the pool.
Your hair might be carried off
by swallows. Hair swirled

around her navel, like water
over a deep hole, softer
than a light wind on my lip.
We never spoke of that, and now

bloodstained grass
is growing on her grave,
a whole crop in one night
when I dare sleep sober

and alone. So—
one glass and two insomnias,
one beer and two legs running,
carrying my gun. Yes,

I saw her death from far away.
It came from the sky in a swarm of bees,
a black thumbprint
closing her startled eyes.

Under my bed the desert
gathers a slow, hot storm.
In the mirror,
which I have turned to the wall,

you look like her. Your hair
is honey-colored, your breast
the size of my hand. Come nearer.
Draw a circle of silence

around me with your tongue.
Don't fear—that hum
is just the bees
straining against the dark walls around them."

5. Ramat Gan

In the valley of your enemy, heat lays
its hand like a poisoned flower
on your face. Old woman, servant

of another old woman. Your breasts
like bags of onions
swing in the faded garden

of your dress, brown
as onions or the hands
you serve me with—

fruit and cold soup—
brushing away from my plate
vines pushing through the window

Ramat Gan is an affluent suburb of Tel Aviv.

with your tattooed wrist. And the man
and children in the photograph
behind you on the wall?

The flag is foreign, flying
on the wrinkled sky, and not quite
out of sight behind it

rolls your memory—a line
of low hills, each topped
with barbed wire, in each dip a grave.

You don't look back,
but I do. And this is what I see:
a woman, just past dawn,

who walks, dripping,
wrapped in an old bedsheet,
to this house from the sea.

Her breasts shock no one.
Her thin legs
beat the pavement like a drum.

You do not fear the thousand
bodies of your enemies
piled like sandbags all around

the thick walls of this house:
they themselves are proof
that in their shadow you are safe.

Not even the smell disturbs you,
screened as it is by boughs
of eucalyptus bowing at this door.

In an Arab Town
West Bank

The fat, pale proprietor
stands at his plateglass window
while we drink tea
with sugar, tea with rum
from our pockets—
none of the men refuse.
It makes them
brave, so they reach out,
delicately at first,
for my white skin,
for whose sake also
two Israeli soldiers
loiter in the street. In fact

we don't talk politics
but Persian verse. I learn,
fighting fingers off my knee,
that no poem should be read
in haste, or carried in a pocket
close to the body's heat. The poet
is the tongue of God's voice. His words
should be recorded in script,
and not by a woman
because her hand will shake.

Then one boy, whose manhood
barely shadows his lip,
recites the perfect letters
which he has placed in my lap.
They teach us *mabrook*,
"you are blessed,"
and *fucka*, because all things
are pure to the tongue.

And two girls
who won't come into the teahouse,
who wear so many colors
their men go blind,
pass fruit through the kitchen windows
for us, giggling. Sisters.
We're told they can't read.

But women, we've been warned,
are most dangerous.
Men lose their tempers, their cool,
spread talk, get caught.
Women are perfectly capable
of riding buses,
arms full of chickens and bombs,
giggling all the way
about some fat unmarried neighbor
or some poor man's cock.

"The rich don't have children . . ."

*The Six-Day War was easy.
It's the seventh day that's hard.*
—ISRAELI SAYING

The rich don't have children
because of the expense,
the lazy because they're lazy,
and the sad because of wars.

Here that's especially true.
The rich go to America,
the lazy die,
and all the sad are drafted.

Fine soldiers, these boys.
They stay awake all night at the gate
keeping the dark orchard at bay. And they love

to walk through Old Jerusalem, inspecting
every one of her widening cracks
for bombs. A fine lady, Jerusalem,

united now with her lover,
her other self.
No more love letters.
No more smuggled children to be raised
by the dark sisters outside the wall.

"No rape at all?" said a French correspondent,
shaking his head. "What kind of army is that?"

"I'm sorry," said the Arab girl, "but it is true."

"I'm sorry," said the paratrooper
who gave me a lift to Bethlehem.
"We can't do everything. We are so few."

At the Wailing Wall

Between stones, weeds
sprout out and down. Paper
is rolled, spit-balled, folded
in all the cracks: prayers
for peace and babies. The old Jews,
costumed like Polish businessmen,
circa 1800, dip and bob—
intense, oblivious
to cameras, shouts,
and paper yarmulkes. We take turns
posing and photographing, touch the Wall,
test the weeds, are not quite
crass enough
to unroll prayers and read them. These Jews

can't drink, dance, gamble,
or touch a woman. What they can do
is smoke—when the Law was given
Columbus hadn't sailed.
We say they bob at the Wall
trying to light up in the wind,
hiding butts and matchbooks
in the stone. We blaspheme, of course,

from opposite sides of the barrier.
You're back-to-back with a Jew in black.
Your hand's on the Wall, the other's
in the pocket of your lambskin coat.
Busy thanking God you weren't born
female. And the soldiers

are happy to pose: green fatigues
and M-16s, that walnut tan that means
they've faced the Wall's white glare
for months, the sun nearly blinding
their search for bombs and paint.
I want to scrawl,
"God was here!" Instead

I scribble something on a matchbook,
pocket it. The soldiers wave. I grin,
walk backwards up the steps,
snap you, the soldiers, and the Wall,
with—higher up—
the Golden Dome of Islam
bright with ice.

Bargaining
Jerusalem

1.

Tug the embroidered sleeve
of your famous coat.
A bit too small, but easy
for the boy to track us here,
the price down *for you my friend*
not enough.

He squats on the doorstep in sun.
Will he tell the carpet man
we stopped, took pictures
in the food street? (A patch of sun
by the bananas, the skinned dromedary heads
too much in shadow.)

We'd like to sit here all day
drinking tea and saying things like
"Absence of violence is luxury," and
"Isn't it funny the streets are never sunny,"
while the price comes down on its own.

2.

"You would like something more than tea?"

"Tea is fine."

"You are not hungry?"

"Tea is fine."

"What is wrong with your woman?
She smokes opium, yes?
There is something wrong with her eyes, yes?"

"Opium? My friend!"

Right hand over your left lapel,
four inches above your heart.

"You would like to do some business?"

Your hands on the table.

"My friend, I would like to do some business,
but you have insulted my friend."

"This is very nice coat.
This coat is from Jerusalem?"

His fingers on the lamb of your lapel.

"This coat is from Afghanistan."

"Afghanistan? I know this place.
How much do you pay?"

Your fingers, soft from sweating,
round from fever.

"Thirty dollars."

"Thirty dollars you pay in Afghanistan?
This is too much."

"This coat is all lambskin.
Thirty dollars is not too much."

"You are rich man?"

"No, I am not a rich man."

"Come. I show you my jewelry.
You buy some for this woman."

"We will come maybe later."

"Later maybe I close."

Your hands deep in your pockets.

"We will come tomorrow."

"Tomorrow, maybe it rains."

3.

The street of the Bedouin,
of jewelry, Kalashnikovs,
and small embroidered vests,
more expensive than dresses,
than guns.
Each woman in her lifetime sews many dresses
but only one embroidered vest, displayed
on the day of her marriage. Fifty dollars
if you're clever. One hundred fifty
if you're not.

In the teahouse, all women
sit in the second room.
The smell of dung and cinnamon
clings to my sleeves and hair.
I rest my legs on the seat
of an empty chair, open my book
and pretend to read, secretly examining
the white scuff on my boot—

the donkey didn't weigh much
even loaded with meat.
I must learn at least to recognize the Arabic
for Get the fuck out of the way.

And the waiter lingers.
Can I read?
Can I afford to buy?
I finger the mint leaves out of my glass,
put them on my tongue. The tongue,

the penis, and the brain—all
concentrations of nerve and blood.
And the finger tips. And the linings
hidden under intricate design.

My legs are strong and too long.
A woman must be thin to wear
such a tiny, singular vest.

4.

Light a cigarette. You can hurry
later. The carpet man smiles.

"My friend, three countries come and go."
He counts them on his three smallest fingers.

"Now see: all camel hair. I show you with a match."
The hair curls and yellows slow: no cotton.

His boy serves tea on a brass tray.
The price down forty pounds.

And which of the three is best, old man?

"O my friend!" He touches his head,
a way they show they are religious men.

5.

In the Church of the Holy Sepulchre
at a hole in the back of the crypt
a bearded monk pulls me down

till my knees warm two small ovals
on the damp rock floor

to squint past a hundred-watt bulb
at layers of black and white stone
he explains in English only as
"Black, see, and white,"

and fills my unwilling hand
with *Mater Dolorosa M. Calvari* postcards
by Miland, and holy water. I leave

with two cold knees, a sticky palm,
and red marks where his fingers got my wrist.

6.

A coffee vendor stops,
stooped under his brass contraption. Hey!
Afghani man!
Hashish man!

We look down the Valley of Kidron.
Judgment trumpet's going to blow
right here, the graveyards full
of Jew, Christian, Muslim,
everyone sleeping first in line.

There's snow on the Golden Dome.
Steam frosts the coffee-vendor's hair.
We walk away.

Two soldiers nod,
we walk away. And, Hey!

You-a-tourist
can-I-help-you
shall-I-fuck-you
give-you-hash?
We walk away. Their shoes

follow. We short-cut into the food street,
buy cheese, pita.
Little boys in short pants
duck behind loaded donkeys, shout
Hey! Americans! run.

We walk away.

The Hands in Exile
for K.C.

It's true there is no one to say how many sparrows per branch
or how many branches obscure the road. My thighs
want something of that, a foreign mystery splashing up.
Now my hands are tired. They have prepared the meals and lifted
the artifacts and bags over a hundred thresholds,
and they say they want only letters, alphabets,
insignias of every sort, ands and ampersands
and fractions, a voice clattering as hooves.
It is they that are Alexandria and islands now.
And you ask me to wear my hair like the smells in old cities,
old as the art of cutting stone: Shamir,
the worm that cuts the cotton
and rots the stone. And now when you trade
it is not for the pearl but for the sand,
schedule of trains, street names,
addresses stolen for no reason. Ignore the dreams.
There are others, dampness
even in a climate like this. Want finally
to take shelter in a doorway of a street
just wide enough for a train of donkeys to pass.

Volunteers

The smell of my son is like
the smell of a fertile field
newly blessed by Yahweh.
—GENESIS 27:27

Three things only are impersonal:
insomnia, land mines, and long hours of work.
Everything else is ours or not ours,
divided like the world
inside and outside the skin.

Walking in the evenings, we see the dead
on both banks of the stream
standing with their children.
But we do not approach.

    When God told Jacob
    "Don't touch this stone,
    bone of my body,"
    Jacob made an altar
    by throwing all stones
    into a single ditch.
    That's how he cleared his fields.

    And God rewarded him.
    He sent the worm, Shamir,
    whose puffy body
    purified all it touched.
    Everything that rotted,
    after that, was holy.

"A trick I learned," said Jacob,
"to fool my father with food,
  to worship with my plow,
  to win the angel's blessing
fighting back."

And these are Jacob's fields.
Hard and flat, the soil must be held
like dry meat in the mouth
before it yields. The pure
are useless. We walk

and the dead, with all their documents,
stand still. The chill
is all that's left of a day's sweat,
a white powder
we brush away from our arms.

            The gardens of peace—
            we left when the gates were open.
            The garden of sweat—
            we eat our meals here
            with an appetite and thirst.

Part Two

Mare

Her eyes turn outward
like two streams of water.
Straight ahead
is a sacred blind spot.
I stand there while she dozes.

A bird flying left to right
vanishes over this dark island,
then reappears, flying low, hunting.

When a mouse dies in this shadow
its spirit emits an odor
of camomile, a prairie drying
from the inner sides of my thighs.

When one mare births
another stands close by.
She listens.
She opens her nostrils
to the cool slide of wind
that carries the coyote's feet
into her lungs.

Her skin, twitching
under the pirouette of a fly,
is damp and sweet and elastic.
My clumsy hands
stick. They are welcome there.

My skin is air
trapped in a breeze.
And the mask I sketch in sleep
has two eyes turning outward
like the hands of an Indian prayer.

Sauna

for Steve

In the smell of pine and fire
we sweat. We hear it drip
and hiss around the stove.
We don't talk.

Dead wood. Low sun. The river
almost frozen shut. The road—
my hands were numb on the wheel.
"Cruelty," you kept saying,
"you don't know anything about it.
Don't flatter yourself."
           I cut the curves.
Slush fanned up from the puddles.
"Turn here! Turn here!" Wipers,
left, a steep, worn-out pavement,
over the crest a town,
the church the only thing painted
in twenty years, a café.
           I drank tea.
"You never hurt my feelings,"
you mumbled into corned beef,
blueberry pie, and Muzak.
"You were in over your head,
that's all."
           We angled east
and put the heater on. The highway
cut between the iced-up rocks below us.
           "You've been kind,"
you whispered, "Kind."
           My foot went down.
Slush and potholes hurled us downhill,
flashed my bare trees, cattails,
each with a blackbird. "Look,
the river's high.
It's spring soon."

Three colorless ducks
go over, land beyond the trees. Below me
you turn over once. My sweat
makes a dull noise falling on your skin.

Altitude
for R.

Not even by climbing
can I get away from you.
Ten thousand feet you'd
think would do it. Who
are you, anyway? No man
I ever knew was this
persistent, no arms
no legs ever held me
like this.
             Way back
when I thought I knew you
you used to say
that when you talked about others
it was you, really, but
when you talked about yourself it was me, and when
you went to the mountains
it was to get rid of
all of us. It was
all very complicated and
untrue.
             Coming down
the mountain that day
you said, "Please don't ever
touch me again. It
makes my balls hurt, makes
my head spin, makes me
not sure I want
what I really want."
And later, on the stairs, you
pressed your thighs together
and said, "Oh God
don't let a woman enter
this dream."

Sitting here
in Indian summer at ten
thousand feet I wish
we were as unsubstantial
as you seemed. Am I
the only one not surprised
that when we step
out of our bodies, our
bodies are the ones
to rise?

Dreams of a Man without Children
for P.

Sometimes her sleep walks in a body
out of the room,
out to the wide green lawn
where images of animals stand
with the trees among them.
And one is a bird without wings.

I don't trust her sleep. It never speaks.
I see a wing that opens like a hand
and is empty.
But it can't be a wing, alone. It's a cell
or a root, some thing that needs no other.

I tell her it is painless, only
a mute, white tearing underground.
But her sleep always answers:
the cell divides and breaks its rope
and leaps into the body of a tree.

So I dream about the words.
I see them even when waking, snakes
attached to everything
going back to the ground.
I want to take the body of her sleep
by force, but then I dream she wakes
while her sleep still carries that sound.

It comes into the room and lifts her by the hand.
They hold a box between them.
Out in the images of trees, they set it down.
Her sleep climbs in. My wife follows.
I watch, unable to speak.
My hands have disappeared.
Animals come
standing in a circle on the lawn.

Zen

In the dark the discipline
was easy. Like the fine edge
of lilies in silhouette
it was there unseen,
the thing without which
there would be no lilies,
only light
unbound by color
and constant,
no score of minute motions
raising in the hidden tubes
each precious drop to the bloom.

Travel

Normally I walk everywhere.
My legs get used to depending on each other.
In the seams of my clothes,
in doorways, I am always looking.

"Come in," says
 one landlady after another.
"Pasa. Bienvenido." And their hands
 flutter near mine like common insects,
 hardworking and entirely visible.
 One kind eats the other
 and that is nature.

"You start," said a man on a plane.
"And then you start again."
 I do this in order
 to have a long way to go.
 And something is always beckoning, an ocean
 in the eyes of a man
 in a bar in a land-locked town.

How many times have I entered heaven
this way? And backed out.
And entered again,
two feet at a time,
selling myself each day
with legs opening, closing.

I try, at night,
to buy myself back with this pen.
It doesn't weigh much.
It can't write in the rain.
So I keep my mouth open
as if it were hard to breathe.
I might catch something on my tongue.

Two legs and one pen.
"Ven! Ven!" shout the landladies,
louder and louder
because I do not understand:

Here are clocks
by which I am already old.
And here are minutes in which
all gold is the gold of my hair.

Life Cycle of the Pacific Mermaid

On this rock, awash in blonde hair like sin,
my breasts grow like sponges. Men say
I'll soak them for all they've got.
It isn't much—a necklace of fingernails.
Souls don't last in this air.

They imagine me white-skinned,
a mouth circular, kissing air like a fish.
They want daughters out of me, pale girls
they can paint red, train to swim through air.

Most of them are beat to death on the rocks,
but I give them their offspring, anyway:
in a sea of sperm I loose my eggs.
The hatchlings, with thick membranous toes,
are sexless, musical, kind.

Those who survive the slow gelling,
the sand crabs and gulls,
climb to their fathers' houses
and wait for thumbs to grow.
Soon their brothers are out here.

I admit it's a good trick,
waiting for moon to whiten my skin.
They walk right into the tide.
Holding my breath in the air, I just watch,
and scratch my green hide on this rock.

No Matter
for Michael

No matter how many years there are
there are always weeks:
the official attitude of your left hand.

At the kitchen table you can
beat any man alive
fighting fucking or running a foot race.

Another month. The moon dips out of the roof
its cup-full, the thermometer
slips toward duplicity. *C'est septembre!*

you shout in mid-December
and the cat you can't afford
pauses at its bowl.

Behind the paper bags
the chewing mice arrange
for their little mice-to-be

while two worlds
between your eyelids
lie toppled on their sides. Outside

in the dry, nutritious footprint of the sea
snow is growing. How ambitious.
Come on. It's only Tuesday. By Friday

your quadrumanous jig
will start. Now how your hair aches
watching me shave my foot.

Talking from Inverness

Mid-stream, midtown, a man in waders
slow-motions toward the bridge, his Hardy
bent by a transparent mouth. Your voice
wavers. Under water
the cables bow. What season
is it? Bass? Most of the country's
private. Poor men
fish in the city. I watch them
when it's raining, or, like now,
the sun sets on Craig Phadrig.
It's midnight here. What?
It means the Crag of Patrick, Saint
I guess, but maybe not.
You say I'm talking Scottish.
You're talking with your mouth full.

And doing? I'm just sitting,
one leg out the window in the rain.
The city duplicates at dusk:
the inner world is shining up,
the modern shining down. Midstream,
two men stand knee-to-knee. The lower one
does headstands on the sun. His wife
is prob'ly pissed. If he's not drinking,
then he's fishing. That's all
this sun is good for. Salmon
's what he's after. Whose wife? Oh
the man's, of course, the man's.

A Meditation in Perthshire, Scotland

Through my sleeping bag I hear cows
tear grass, grind teeth,
blow pollen out their noses.
They leave me alone. Six miles from here,
three hundred and thirty years ago,
an ancestor of mine was born
to the third short marriage of a woman
who owned nothing but a farm.
Last century an anthropologist
bribed a hundred of her people
to let him measure their skulls,
bone lengths, dark hair, all unchanged
since they were subjects of Canatulachma
eighteen centuries ago.
They still loved poetry and their land,
suspected the anthropologist
of unnatural motives. These
were people hunted with dogs.
Six of their heads bought pardon for a crime.
Their names were changed
by law. They fell, slowly,
for a hundred and fifty years
into the fogs of Rannoch, Trossachs, America.

I come out of my sleeping bag. The cows
startle back to the fence.
No, I'm neither dark nor small.
I have no friends named Bliesblituth.
I see the way a stone lies
on the dirt or on the grass: how nearly
I didn't exist. I see it this way:
sleds of flowers
are delivered to the houses of survivors. A Bible
was written in London the same year
those women who weren't my mother

were delivered by Caesarean, by sword,
from their mothers into the literal snow.

The cows have never seen a human bed before.
Grass hangs mixed with spit from their lips
as I brush my hair. Yesterday
I toured a castle
whose stone looked soft as skin. Inside
the document of genocide was displayed
as an artifact
by the small, dark descendant of the sword.
His arm, thank God,
isn't strong enough to swing it. His people, too,
still love poetry and land. Those sleds of flowers—
I mean it. Yesterday
I paid admission to a castle
to see my name changed: *Diteadh gu bas*—
"condemned to death." Today
I'll walk six miles to a farmyard,
accept lemonade from a woman half my size.
The men will mow. We'll rest our backs
against the fence and watch
the flashing blades, the larks
that flush up from the hay.

October

The first morning of chickadees.
New skin grows on the windows
and on the leaves
impacted in the yard—

for a month they ran loose,
now they sleep.

On the dirt of the plowed-under garden
every clod's a crystal. I break ice
to scatter seed, and finches
—those earnest roses—
bloom like thoughts, sudden

and where they don't belong.
The seasons change like news
from another country:
somewhere north a wind god
sharpens his cold, clear blade.

But here, a thin dust. Mud
forms wide black footprints
where I step, a fixed trail
whose outline will vanish in a day.

There! A blue-bright jay
lands on the mailbox. Snow crystals
shoot light from his head, like memory
opening its eye in the mind—

a solemn eye, great narcissus,
white and calm in the cold air.
Through its trumpet everything
passes, compressed to crystal. Snow

is all I will remember,
its soft cap on the cows,
ice on the ponies' whiskers.
When I open my jacket—
brief needles on my collarbones.

No, I have never traveled.
I've always been here, upside down
on a ball of roots, hair and thoughts
all tangled up in dirt. This morning

there is no wind. There is no news.
There is no other country.
Dirt throws off its colors,
and the ridges

are stunned to silence by the lakes
which look, from above,
like a chain of precious stones,
cool and priceless at earth's warm neck.

Florida Scott-Maxwell Helps Recite My
Grandmother's Life

In bloom on the logging road:
wild rose, Indian paintbrush,
and a three-petaled white one. Trouble
turning pages in the flower book.
The grandchildren say,
"Why not get a new one?"
I think the flowers haven't changed.
He called me his wild rose.

When I was a child I went with my grandfather
when he hunted wild turkey or quail,
driving through the roadless woods
under great water oaks, shining
as though newly washed by rain.
Once, near a river,
I jumped from the wagon,
ran into the deep shade,
and sat down on a large
alligator. I was also the child

hiding books in the parlor. "Reading,"
Father would whisper. "Not
dusting." And the terrible hush in the parlor
when Ethel came. Ethel
brought books, ivory elephants,
Mexican donkeys made of straw, glass dogs
from China. Ethel
made my daughter rich
ten years after my death
with real blue-willow Chinese
china. Ethel, my aunt,
(whisper: *all concrete accomplishment belongs to men*)
lives like a man
or
lives with a man

or, my mother asks,
"How *is* Rebecca? And why
should two women so attractive
never marry, live together, read so much?"

When you truly possess all you have been and done . . .
(Possess: to have as property, quality,
mastery, or control.
To have sexual intercourse with.
To seize (Middle English).
Latin: to sit as master,
to sit down.
See Appendix: *sed:* to sit, set, saddle.
Lengthened grade form: residence.
In Greek: *piezo:* to press tight.) Possess

then, in an armchair, covetously,
the past. And then
to let it all go. Or,
rather, take it,
the children growing up without it.
We have the page now: Virgin's Star, a
three-petaled (*Lithophragma parviflorum*) white one.
He called me his wild rose.

But still
fool that I am, I worry at life
like a dog with an old shoe: my daughter,
the children all lined up on their ponies.
I do come out and take a look. In fact,
I watch them every Saturday, over little fences,
their tense knees. *It is baffling to be loved*
by someone incapable of seeing you. They see me bent
and generous with fear. "A quarter for ice-cream?"
"A safety pin for my sleeve?" Mammaw.

My only fear about death
is that it will not come soon enough.
I've seen death once or twice.
My father drawing bead on a maddened horse.

My uncle lying calmly in the parlor, me
tugging his sleeve for a game of whist.
That other uncle—a photograph from Phoenix
with a mustache and a pony and a gun.
The doctor's letter:
he was respected and admired by all who knew him,
a rare man. And Ethel. The mad artist
she kept in her last years
hid the bacon and the silver
on the roof. Finally, the smell of it
led us to it, led, in truth,
my son-in-law to it,
up in the pigeon-shit, slate-tile
mess of a roof of her elegant Georgetown
house. *It hardly matters whether I am*
mortal or not. She left him
everything but the china.

The grandchildren
look at the flower in the old book,
show me the flower in the new book. So I say,
"Listen more often to the trees. They tell you
when it will rain." "Why is it called
an Indian paintbrush, Mammaw?"
                              I remember
a wagon pulled all by mares, each of them
thick with foal, a wagon
of Christmas hams and bracelets.
We bartered with the Chippewa for rice—
we were that far north. He was an architect.
Trees came in board-feet into my dreams.
I was mad to uproot.

It is (I remember now)
faintly disgusting
to marry at thirty-six, and worse
to bear a child. ("It will kill her
and her poor mother, too.")
The child seemed to claim
almost all my body. I held on, wondering
if my burden was my enemy. But I was

his wild rose, his Scottish rose, and the child
fell from us like a fragrance before we
wilted. "And why can I not have a brother?"
she asks me to this day.

The combat of life. The wireless announcing
war, and all of us rushing off to can corn,
my daughter riding the train
(My daughter is going to college!)
a sailor asleep on each shoulder.

                    I see myself still
in his post offices, his plans: Sioux Falls, Dearborn,
St. Cloud, Rosebud Sioux, most of them now themselves
replaced. *I do not know if it is a sad thing or
a solace to be past change.*

I go and I make myself tea.
I put away clean linens.
I water my plants. *Order.*
Cleanliness. Seemliness.
To live at last
like a humble but watchful ghost.
I am almost free. Almost.
My nonexistence makes me
spacious. *We may each die from being ourselves.*

I will die, I hope, before this
granddaughter, seventeen, explodes
like the red heart of a willow in spring flood.
"I could neaten the stars," she'll say
as I put my possessions in order.
  And when my daughter says to her,
"Go ahead and cry, honey," she'll
straighten, wipe her nose, go outside,
say nothing more about it.

Can I make it total
to a quiet heart? I am
a miracle of quiet. I am,

pressed close, a miracle of
possession, of
being more than ourselves.
The beat of life. We all must look at
a garden, cat, fire. But
already the habit of "we"
is going. "They" become "I," and "one"
wants shelter. *When you tell me*
what I could have been . . .
So be it. In bloom
today on the logging road: wild rose.

The Soul in the Valley of Kidron

I woke up once and saw the sky
balanced on a vee of dry white hills
like a jewel on the tips
of two silver fingers, all this
wrapped about the finger
of a woman. God of Abraham,

how I want a woman! The smell of the air
was so much like her skin. Even the trees
smelled like pockets of hair
between her legs, under her arms
—arms that turned to vineyards in the dark.
And her breasts were always cool
like mountains standing
in thin, perfected air.

Next, I listened. What
had awakened me? Not even
the pressure of a lip
against the lip of a horn.
It was not dawn, not dusk.
There was no place anyone
was asking me to go. Not even

guns as I remember them,
mouthing my nerves like lions.
Gabriel, I imagine,
was not even nearby at the time.
I couldn't move. A white stone
lay on my chest like armor.
And I could not feel.

I pressed down on the earth,
its grains, its leaves,
its little pointed sticks—
it wasn't there, or else
I was alive and dreaming
so I could fall and fall
but never strike.

I breathed in deep. I am
supposed to do that, I remember,
to let the eucalyptus clear my heart.
But Rabbi, how can I repent me of the earth
when down from every hillside flies
the olive with its green bells ringing
and its odor of an unwashed shirt?

NOTES

Part One

PAGE 6 *Justine* is the first novel of Lawrence Durrell's *Alexandria Quartet.*

26 The Huleh Valley—the biblical Waters of Merom, battlefield of Joshua against the Northern Canaanites—was, until well into this century, a mass of pools, swamps, and channels, given over to wildlife and malaria. Swamp drainage and the straightening and deepening of the Jordan River bed have reclaimed it for agricultural use.

28 Italicized passage: John 12:24.

31 The Irgun Zvai Leumi was an underground Jewish organization in Palestine that pursued Israeli independence with the bomb and gun. Characterized by all but their own as terrorists and murderers, the Irgun, with its emblem of a brandished rifle and its motto, "Only Thus," was a key factor in Great Britain's decision to abandon its Palestine mandate. Irgun members went on to responsible positions in Israeli armed forces, government, and intelligence.

34 Quoted passage is adapted from Natan Alterman's "The Silver Tray," available in English in *Poems from the Hebrew,* selected by Robert Mezey and published by Thomas Y. Crowell Company, New York.

37 War broke out between Israel and her neighbors on Yom Kippur, the Day of Atonement, 1973.

43 "Identity Card" is the title of a poem by Mahmoud Darwish, a Palestinian poet living in exile. It refers to the card all Palestinian Arabs in Israel must carry.

52 A green banner is the battle standard of Islam.

54 In 1974 Palestinian guerrillas protested Richard Nixon's visit to Israel by attacking Kibbutz Shamir. One volunteer, several kibbutzniks, and all the terrorists were killed.

PAGE 57   The west bank of the Jordan River was controlled by Jordan from 1949 until 1967. It has been occupied by Israel since the Six-Day War.

59   For nineteen years the city of Jerusalem was administered by two hostile powers—the western, modern sector by Israel, and the eastern, ancient sector by Jordan. East Jerusalem was captured by Israeli troops in 1967 after bitter fighting. Israelis consider Jerusalem, in its entirety, to be their capital.

60   The Wailing Wall is the western wall of Jerusalem's second temple, and, as such, is the holiest site of the Jews. The remainder of the temple lies beneath the foundations of two of Islam's holiest sites—El Aqsa Mosque and the Dome of the Rock. Beneath the Dome is the rock where Isaac was spared. Later, the last earthly footprint of Mohammed was left on this rock as the prophet ascended into paradise.

64   The Kalashnikov is a Russian-made, semiautomatic rifle, comparable to the M-16.
Italicized passage is from a tourist pamphlet.

65   The three countries referred to are Great Britain, Jordan, and Israel.

65   The Church of the Holy Sepulchre, erected by the Crusaders, enshrines one of the possible tombs of Jesus.

66   The Valley, or Wadi, of Kidron, the biblical site of Judgment Day, is primarily a place of burial.

Part Two

83   Italicized passage is from *Crooner's Party,* a novel by Michael O'Hanlon.

85   During the nineteenth century, the anthropologist John Beddoe reported that the genetic pool of the central Scottish highlands had remained essentially unchanged from late Pictish times until the dawn of the industrial age. From the fourteenth century on, the lands and rights of these ancient Pictish clans were violently infringed upon by their increasingly powerful neighbors—clans of British, Scandinavian, and Irish-Gael descent. Emigration to the New World, Australia, and South Africa was a major factor in saving some of these peoples from extinction.
My ancestors were MacGruders (of Clan Gregor) of the region around

Crieff. The document of genocide ("proscription") against Clan Gregor was signed by King James, VI of Scotland and I of England, in 1603. Canatulachma was a Pictish king, Bliesblituth a Pictish name.

89 Florida Pier Scott-Maxwell was an American-born actress, writer, wife, mother, and suffragette. At the age of fifty she began the study of analytical psychology under Jung, and she later practiced at clinics in Great Britain. Italicized passages are adapted from the published journal of her old age, *The Measure of My Days*, Alfred A. Knopf, Inc., 1968.

Susan Tichy was born in Washington, D.C., in 1952. She received a B.A. from Goddard College and an M.A. from the University of Colorado. Her poems have been published in many magazines, including the *Antioch Review*, *Attaboy!*, the *Beloit Poetry Journal*, *Black Warrior Review* and *Blue Buildings*. She lives in Colorado.